PlayKits

WHOLE LANGUAGE ACTIVITIES
Patterns for dramatic play
by Candy Jones and Lea McGee, illustrated by Marilynn G. Barr

Publisher: Roberta Suid
Editor: Carol Whiteley
Production: Susan Cronin-Paris

Entire contents copyright ©1991 by Monday Morning
Books, Inc., Box 1680, Palo Alto, California 94302

Monday Morning is a registered trademark of
Monday Morning Books, Inc.

ISBN 1-878279-26-2

Printed in the United States of America
9 8 7 6 5 4 3 2 1

For a complete catalog, write to the address above.

Contents

Introduction

Children love to play and pretend. And while they play, they learn. In fact, dramatic play is one of the most important ways in which young children learn. They learn to view the world from another person's perspective. Their fine motor development is encouraged. In addition, dramatic play aids children's cognitive development.

Dramatic play also introduces ideas about reading and writing. Because children have seen their own doctors reading patient charts and writing prescriptions, or watched a waiter write down an order in a restaurant, or seen a parent or friend write a letter on paper or a computer, they will naturally include such reading and writing activities in their own play. Very young children will not, of course, really read or write, but pretending to do so will help them begin to learn about those activities.

What Are PlayKits?

The eight kits in PlayKits are designed to help you prepare dramatic play materials and activities for young children. Each kit—Shopping, Medical, Travel, Auto Repair, Office, Restaurant, Construction, and TV Station—contains an overview of how to use the materials, suggestions for related units and related books, a list of necessary materials, a number of reproducible play patterns, and directions for using the patterns as well as making play props. All the props are easily put together from everyday items and craft supplies. The activities are appropriate for young children in preschools, kindergartens, child care, after-school programs, and at home.

How to Use PlayKits

Begin by gathering the ready-made props and construction materials that are listed for the particular kit. Place the construction materials in a large box or pillowcase. Then assemble the props using the easy-to-follow directions provided. Put the completed props back in the box for storage.

Introduce the kit to the children by talking with them about their related experiences, for example, going to the doctor or dentist's office if you're working with the Medical kit. Bring out the dramatic play props and let the children help you create a play area.

Then play with the children as they use the props in a variety of ways. You will be an important model for how the children interact with the materials.

As the children play, be ready to accept different ways of using the props—the children will be learning and growing as they enjoy working with the materials again and again. Also expect that their "reading" and "writing" will be unconventional; remember, however, that engaging in scribble writing and pretend reading is important for learning how to do the real things. Finally, have fun with the materials and the children—jump in and enjoy the show!

Shopping PlayKit

Overview

The Shopping PlayKit contains the ideas and reproducibles you need to provide your students with exciting shopping play. With the props you and your children gather and make (lists follow), you can easily set up a grocery or specialty store, a shopping mall, even a garage sale.

To create a grocery store, display clean, empty food containers and small household items on boxes or shelves. Use copies of the sale price tag pattern to tag the items with the prices they sell for. Set up a toy cash register on a sturdy cardboard box in a convenient "check-out" area. Provide a number of plastic grocery carts or small wicker baskets to add to the shopping fun.

Then encourage the children to play. They can write down things to buy on their shopping lists (picture lists will work for non-writers), sort coupons, write checks for their purchases, or count out play money. A check-out clerk can ring up purchases at the cash register. A carry-out clerk can bag the groceries in paper or plastic bags and help the customers out of the store.

To create a number of specialty stores or a shopping center (this works for a garage sale, too), display old clothes, shoes, toys, sports equipment, books, and other appropriate items. Encourage the children to decorate large appliance boxes to use as storefronts. The children will enjoy making store signs as well as signs for specials on selected merchandise. Department store catalogs can be displayed with merchandise. Shopping bags from local stores can be used to hold items as they're bought. Shoppers will enjoy using their personalized credit cards to make purchases.

Related Books

Anno's Flea Market by Mitsumasa Anno (Philomel Books, 1984).

Caps for Sale by Esphyr Slobodkina (Harper, 1947).

Corduroy by Don Freeman (Viking, 1968).

Don't Forget the Bacon by Pat Hutchins (Puffin, 1982).

Food Market by Peter Speir (Doubleday, 1981).

General Store by Nancy Winslow (Morrow, 1988).

The Gift by John Prater (Viking, 1986).

MacGoose's Grocery by Frank Asch (Scholastic, 1978).

My Mother Is Lost by Bernice Myers (Scholastic, 1970).

On Market Street by Arnold Lobel (Scholastic, 1982).

Our Garage Sale by Anne Rockwell (Greenwillow, 1984).

The Pet Store by Peter Speir (Doubleday, 1981).

Materials

Ready-made Props

toy cash register and telephone

plastic name badge holders or name tags

hangers

play money

notepads and paper

plastic or paper bags, shopping bags

newspaper advertisement pages, catalogs

clothes-drying racks (for hanging clothes)

coupons

plastic shopping carts or small baskets

pens, pencils, markers

doll strollers, dolls

dress-up clothes (hats, neckties, purses, wallets)

clean, empty food boxes, plastic bottles

small household items (real or toy versions)

variety of old clothes, shoes, toys, books, records, costume jewelry (for garage sale)

Construction Materials

tape

poster board

craft knife, scissors

fabric or old sheet, ribbon, lace, netting

construction paper, white paper, waxed paper

cardboard boxes, appliance boxes

markers, crayons

stapler

laminating materials or clear Contact paper

pan

water

liquid starch

Related Units

Social Living

Nutrition

Food Production

Health and Hygiene

Careers

Money and Counting

Pattern Directions

Sale and Specials Signs: Duplicate the patterns on a number of pieces of construction paper. Cut the signs out or have the children do the cutting. Then encourage the children to write the names or draw pictures on the patterns of the items they want to have on sale.

Sale Price Tag: Duplicate the pattern on construction paper. Cut the patterns out and help the children to write prices on the tags, then tape or hole punch and tie the tags to appropriate items.

Shopping List: Make a large number of copies of the shopping list pattern. Cut them out and staple them together in sets of eight to ten to form pads.

Checkbook: Make a large number of copies of the checkbook pattern. Cut them out and then staple them together in sets of eight to ten to form checkbooks.

Credit Card: Duplicate enough credit card patterns to give one to each child. Cut the patterns out and have the children color the cards and write their names on them. Laminate the cards or cover them with clear Contact paper.

Prop Directions

Name Badges: Gather enough plastic name badge holders or sticky-backed name tags to give one to each child. Help each child to write his or her name on a piece of paper to insert in the holder, or to write the name directly on the tag.

Store Signs: Cut poster board into 9" x 28" signs. Write the name of a store on each sign, then tape the signs to appliance-box storefronts or place them on display shelves.

Counters and Storefronts: Let the children decorate appliance boxes and smaller cardboard boxes to use as storefronts and display counters. Have the children arrange the items for sale on the counters.

Make-a-Hat (Fancy Shopping Hat)

For each hat, cut a 14"-diameter circle from fabric or an old sheet. Cut out and discard a 6"-diameter circle from the center of the fabric circle to form a hat. Dip the hat into a pan containing a mixture of $\frac{1}{4}$ cup water and $\frac{1}{4}$ cup liquid starch. Lay the fabric on a piece of waxed paper to dry. When dry, decorate the hat with ribbon, lace, flowers, or netting.

Signs

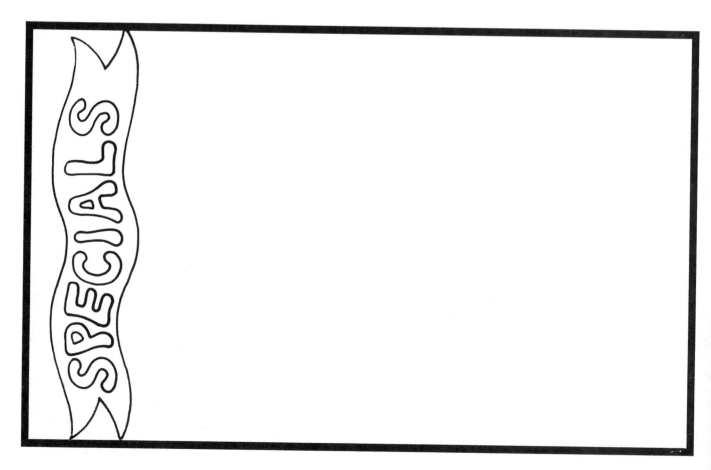

Sale Price Tag

Shopping List

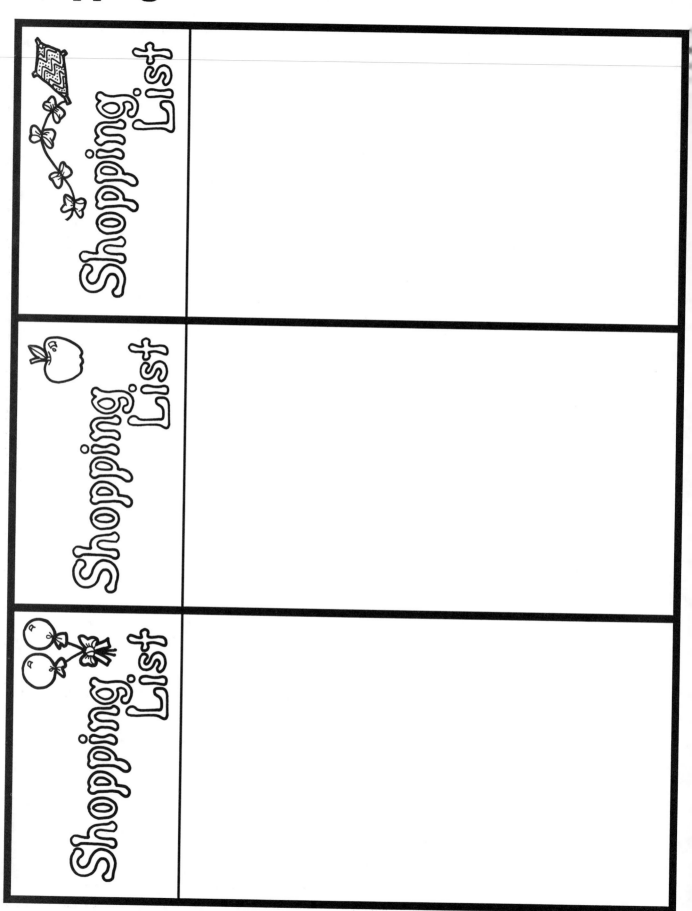

Checkbook

_____ 19 ____

Pay to _____

_____ Dollars

_____

_____ 19 ____

Pay to _____

_____ Dollars

_____

_____ 19 ____

Pay to _____

_____ Dollars

_____

_____ 19 ____

Pay to _____

_____ Dollars

_____

Credit Card

Medical PlayKit

Overview

The Medical PlayKit contains the ideas and reproducibles you need to help your students enjoy creative medical office play. With the materials you and your children gather and make (lists follow), you can easily set up a doctor's, dentist's, or veterinarian's office.

To create a doctor's office, set up a cardboard box to act as a receptionist's desk. Add several chairs and magazines on a small table to the reception area. Spread out a cloth, towel, or paper in an examining room area. Then encourage the children to play; different children can become doctor, patient (adult or child), nurse, and receptionist. The doctor can do such things as examine sick babies, mark information on medical charts, and write prescriptions. Patients can be examined, as well as make appointments and pay bills.

To adapt the doctor's office to a dentist's office, just add a mirror, X-rays and impressions of teeth (available from local dentists), toothbrushes, patients' charts showing drawings of teeth, empty outer boxes of toothpaste, and a folding lawn chair for the dentist's examination chair.

To create a veterinarian's office, add clean, empty bottles or packages of heartworm pills, empty bottles of flea shampoo, animal X-rays (available from local veterinarians), animal skeleton posters, animal care pamphlets, and pet grooming equipment. Children may bring in stuffed animals for patients.

Related Books

Alligator's Toothache by Anne Rockwell (Macmillan, 1982).

Arthur's Eyes by Marc Brown (Atlantic Monthly Press, 1985).

Arthur's Tooth by Marc Brown (Atlantic Monthly Press, 1979).

The Bear's Toothache by David McPhail (Puffin, 1972).

Berenstain Bears Go to the Doctor by Stan and Jan Berenstain (Random House, 1981).

Curious George Goes to the Hospital by H. A. Rey (Houghton Mifflin, 1966).

Doctor Shawn by Petronella Brienburg (Crowell, 1975).

The Hospital Book by James Howe (Crown, 1986).

I Wish I Were Sick Too by Franz Brandenberg (Puffin, 1978).

My Doctor by Harlow Rockwell (Macmillan, 1980).

Nicky Goes to the Doctor by Richard Scarry (Western, 1978).

Sick in Bed by Anne Rockwell (Macmillan, 1982).

Taking My Cat to the Vet by Susan Kuklin (Bradbury Press, 1988).

Materials

Ready-made Props

toy stethoscope, blood pressure gauge, needle, thermometer, tongue depressors

cloth, towel, or paper (for examining area)

large white shirt (doctor's uniform)

bathroom scale

empty medicine bottles, small and large bandages

magazines

file box

pencils, pens, markers, paper

tape measure

X-rays

small flashlight

chairs, tables or cardboard boxes

dress-up clothes

dental office equipment (lawn chair for patients, toothbrushes, teeth impressions, mirror, empty boxes of toothpaste, etc.)

veterinarian office equipment (animal X-rays, animal care pamphlets, empty flea shampoo bottles, etc.), stuffed animals

Construction Materials

tape, tape dispenser

poster board

scissors

markers

12" x 18" white construction paper

file folders

stapler

Related Units

Community Helpers

Safety

Drug Abuse

Pets and Pet Care

The Human Body

Teeth

Pattern Directions

Patient's Chart: Make as many copies of the patient's chart pattern as there are students. Staple each pattern to the inside of a file folder. Write a student's name on each folder.

Prescription Pad: Make a large number of copies of the prescription pad pattern. Cut out the patterns and staple them together in sets of eight or ten to form pads.

Medicine Bottle Label: Make several copies of the medicine bottle label pattern. Cut the patterns apart and place them in a file box or other container. Put a tape dispenser and large, clean, empty medicine bottles nearby. Encourage the children to write labels for the bottles and tape them on.

Height and Weight Chart: Make enough copies of the height and weight chart pattern to give one to each child. Staple each pattern to a file folder and add the children's names.

Checkbook: See the checkbook pattern and its directions in the Shopping kit.

Prop Directions

Sign-In Forms: Staple five pieces of paper together. Write "Please Sign In" at the top of each page.

Eye Chart: On a large poster board, make four rows of letters. Make the letters on the top row the largest, and each row of letters successively smaller.

Make-a-Hat (Nurse's Hat)

Fold a 12" x 18" piece of white construction paper in half. Place the nurse's hat pattern on the fold of the paper as directed on the pattern. Trace, cut out, and unfold. Make a one-inch fold at the base as indicated by the line on the pattern. Fold the top section down and staple together corners A and B.

Patient's Chart

Patient's Name _____

eyes

nose

ears

mouth

heart

temperature

Prescription Pad

Dr. _____

Name _____

Age _____

Address _____

Date _____

Phone _____

Rx

Dr. _____

Name _____

Age _____

Address _____

Date _____

Phone _____

Rx

Dr. _____

Name _____

Age _____

Address _____

Date _____

Phone _____

Rx

Dr. _____

Name _____

Age _____

Address _____

Date _____

Phone _____

Rx

Medicine Bottle Label

_____ Pharmacy

R𝒳 #:   Dr.:

Name:

Instructions:

_____ Pharmacy

R𝒳 #:   Dr.:

Name:

Instructions:

_____ Pharmacy

R𝒳 #:   Dr.:

Name:

Instructions:

_____ Pharmacy

R𝒳 #:   Dr.:

Name:

Instructions:

_____ Pharmacy

R𝒳 #:   Dr.:

Name:

Instructions:

_____ Pharmacy

R𝒳 #:   Dr.:

Name:

Instructions:

_____ Pharmacy

R𝒳 #:   Dr.:

Name:

Instructions:

_____ Pharmacy

R𝒳 #:   Dr.:

Name:

Instructions:

_____ Pharmacy

R𝒳 #:   Dr.:

Name:

Instructions:

_____ Pharmacy

R𝒳 #:   Dr.:

Name:

Instructions:

Height and Weight Chart

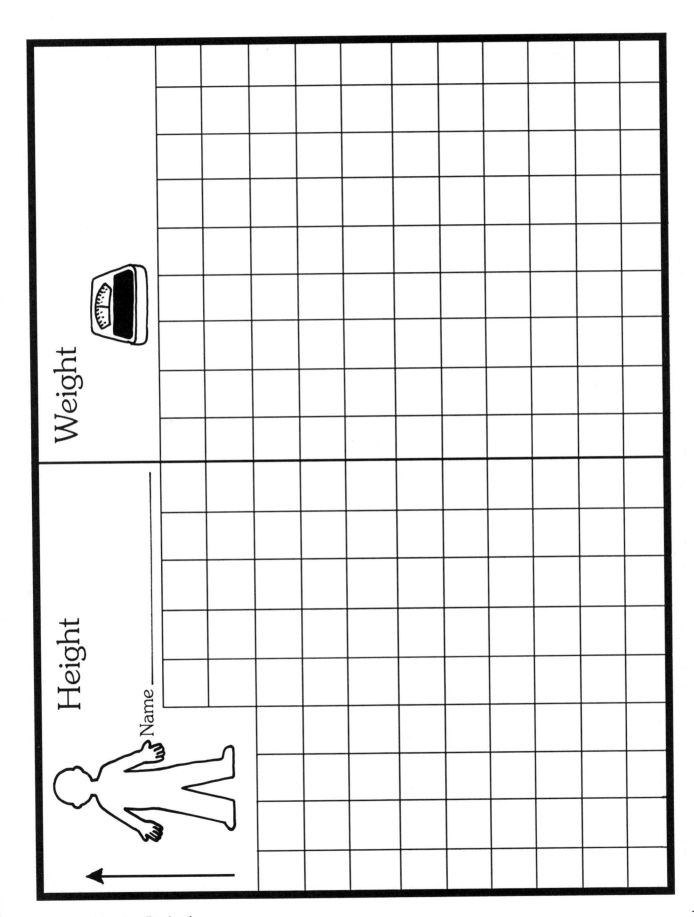

Nurse's Hat

A

B

place on fold →

fold

Travel PlayKit

Overview

The Travel PlayKit includes the ideas and reproducibles you need to provide your students with creative travel play. With the materials you and the children gather and make (lists follow), your class can plan a vacation, then pack their bags and travel to faraway places.

To create a travel agency, place several chairs around a cardboard box desk. Place a toy telephone, travel brochures, paper and pens, envelopes, and several maps on the desk. Display travel posters and post cards on the wall. Old suitcases or tote bags; dress-up clothes; clean, empty toiletry bottles; wallets and purses; and toy cameras should be placed in the housekeeping center or other convenient area.

When everything is set up, encourage the children to play. A travel agent can write tickets, plan trips with maps and brochures, and make passports. Travelers can pack suitcases, tagging them with personalized luggage tag patterns; pretend to visit a foreign country, ski down a mountain, go to a beach, or sleep in a motel; and write post cards home about their adventures.

Some vacationers might travel around in a train, airplane, boat, bus, or car. Let the children draw pictures of some of the places they've visited to stick on the suitcases.

Related Books

Airport by Byron Barton (Crowell, 1982).

Beach Days by Ken Robbins (Viking, 1987).

Clifford Takes a Trip by Norman Bridwell (Scholastic, 1985).

Curious George at the Railroad Station by Margaret Rey (Houghton, 1988).

Freight Train by Donald Crews (Greenwillow, 1978).

How to Travel with Grownups by Elizabeth Bridgman (Crowell, 1988).

I Spy on Vacation by Maureen Roffey (Macmillan, 1988).

Just Me and My Dad by Mercer Mayer (Goldencraft, 1977).

Little Fox Goes to the End of the World by Ann Tompert (Crown, 1976).

My Mom Travels a Lot by Caroline Bauer (Frederick Warne, 1981).

Robot on Vacation by Hildegarde H. Swift (Harcourt, 1988).

Round Trip by Ann Jonas (Greenwillow, 1983).

Something Queer on Vacation by Elizabeth Levy (Bell, 1982).

The Train to Grandma's by Ivan Gantschew (Picture Book Studios, 1987).

Materials

Ready-made Props

small suitcases and tote bags

dress-up clothes, including sunglasses and straw hats

empty toiletry containers, shaving kits, curlers, toothbrushes, shower caps

towels, washcloths

purses, wallets

pens, post cards, paper, envelopes

cardboard mailbox

toy telephone, old telephone books (from several cities)

old cameras or toy cameras

dolls, doll strollers

diaper bag, bottles, diapers

travel brochures, maps (for road, water, and air travel), posters

empty suntan lotion containers

Construction Materials

cardboard box

white and other colors of construction paper, tagboard, poster board, felt

yarn, plastic twist ties

adhesive address labels

markers, crayons

tape, glue

scissors or craft knife, hole punch, stapler

leg warmers or large socks

needle and thread

Related Units

Geography

Economics

Families

Leisure Activities

Transportation

Pattern Directions

Ticket: Duplicate the ticket pattern on a number of sheets of construction paper. Cut the patterns out, or have the children cut them out. Encourage the children to write their names and draw pictures of their travel destinations on the tickets.

Luggage Tag: Duplicate the luggage tag pattern on several pieces of tagboard. Cut the patterns out and punch a hole at the end of each tag. Encourage the children to write their names and addresses on the tags. The tags can be attached to suitcases by slipping a twist tie through the hole and securing it to the suitcase handle.

Passport: Duplicate the passport pattern on several sheets of construction paper. Cut the patterns apart and ask the children to write their names and draw pictures of themselves in the appropriate places. Help the children with the additional information. Staple the cover over the information page.

Post Card: Duplicate the post card pattern on several sheets of white construction paper. Cut the patterns out and encourage the children to write messages, color the pictures, or draw additional pictures on the cards.

Credit Card: See the pattern and its directions in the Shopping kit.

Prop Directions

Signs: Cut poster board into 9" x 28" sections. On each piece write the name of a travel agency, airline, cruise line, railroad station, or bus station, or encourage the children to think of names.

Stationery: Cut sheets of construction paper into 5" x 11" sheets. Encourage the children to decorate the stationery and then write messages on it. The children can mail their letters in the cardboard mailbox.

Suitcase Stickers: Have the children write the names of travel destinations or draw pictures of travel sights on adhesive address labels. The stickers may then be put on the suitcases and tote bags.

Make-a-Hat (Ski Hat)

For each hat, cut two leg warmers or two large socks in half lengthwise. Sew all the pieces together to form one tube. Gather one end of the tube and tie it with yarn. Trace the ski hat decoration patterns onto felt and cut them out. Have the children glue the patterns to the ski hat.

Ticket

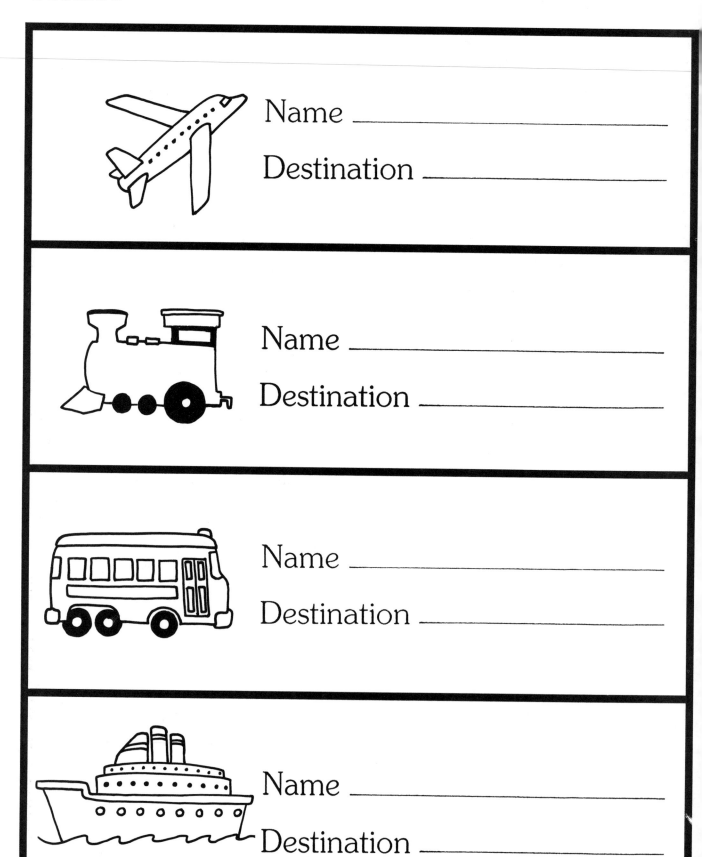

Name _____

Destination _____

Name _____

Destination _____

Name _____

Destination _____

Name _____

Destination _____

24

Luggage Tag

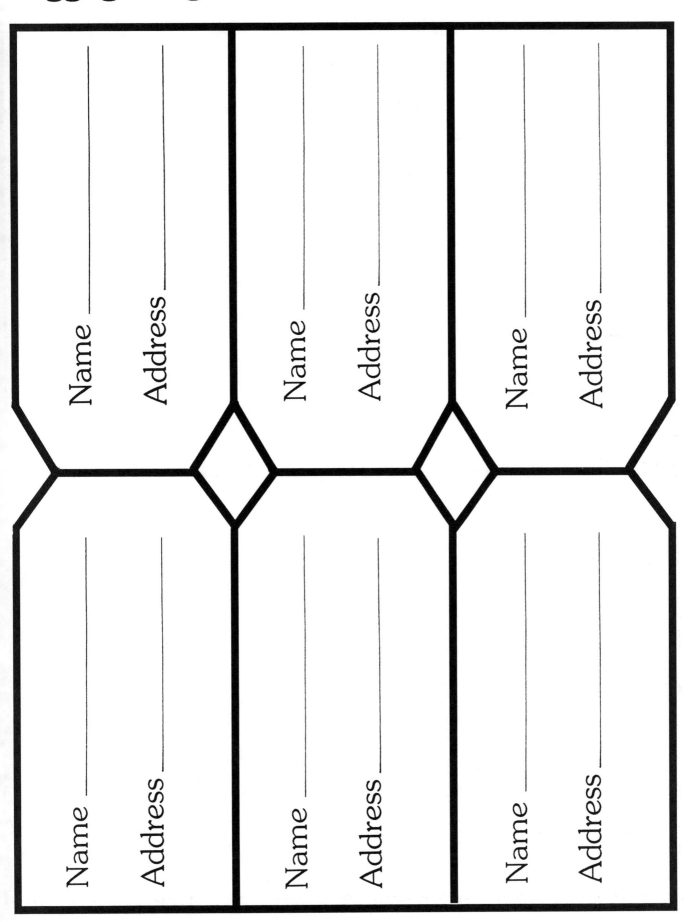

Name

Address

Name

Address

Name

Address

Name

Address

Name

Address

Name

Address

Passport

Name

Address

Country Born In

Height

Weight

Name

Address

Country Born In

Height

Weight

USA

Passport

USA

Passport

Post Card

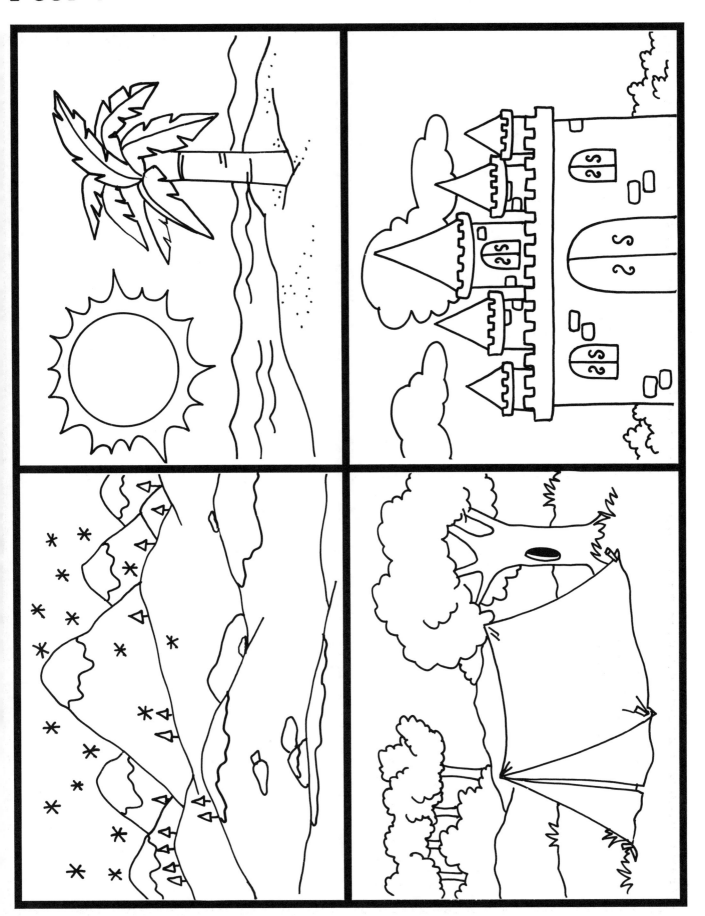

Ski Hat Decorations

28

Auto Repair PlayKit

Overview

The Auto Repair PlayKit provides you with the ideas and reproducibles you need to engage children in enjoyable auto repair shop play. With the materials you and the children gather and make (lists follow), you can set up an auto repair garage as well as a car wash. The kit is especially suitable for outdoor play.

To create a repair shop, display tool chests filled with car repair tools (wrenches, funnels, pliers, etc.); clean, used automobile parts (spark plugs, fan belts, nuts and bolts, etc., available from garages or check with parents); a tire pump and tire repair kit; toy cars and trucks; tricycles, wagons, and scooters. Set up a cardboard box desk to one side of the play area. On it put a toy telephone, paper and pencils, and a clipboard. You can also display auto parts catalogs, warranty books, and new car brochures.

Then encourage the children to play. Customers can drive toy cars and trucks or ride tricycles or bicycles to the garage. Service managers can find out about repair problems and write up claim tickets. Mechanics can check off items on an inspection list, repair vehicles, and make a written or picture list of services completed.

To create a car wash, set out buckets, brushes, sponges, spray bottles, and towels or cloths. Also display clean, empty cans of oil and a tire repair kit. If available, include a toy gas pump. The children will enjoy washing toy cars and tricycles or wagons, fixing flat tires, and pumping gas.

Related Books

Bill's Service Station by Peter Speir (Doubleday, 1981).

The Car: Watch It Work by Ray Marshall (Viking, 1984).

Cars and How They Go by Joanna Cole (Harper & Row, 1983).

Fill It Up! by Gail Gibbons (Holiday House, 1982).

I Read Symbols by Tana Hoban (Greenwillow, 1983).

Machines At Work by Byron Barton (Crowell, 1987).

Monster Trucks & Other Giant Machines on Wheels by Jerry Bucher (Lerner, 1989).

Things On Wheels by Gail Gibbons (Crowell, 1985).

Tool Book by Gail Gibbons (Holiday House, 1982).

The Tool Box by Anne and Harlow Rockwell (Macmillan, 1971).

Tool Chest by Jan Adkins (Walker, 1973).

Truck Song by Diane Silbert (Crowell, 1984).

Trucks by Anne Rockwell (Dutton, 1988).

Trucks You Can Count On by Doug Magee (Dodd, Mead, 1985).

Materials

Ready-made Props

tool chest or tackle box

tools (wrenches, screwdrivers, pliers, funnels, etc.)

used car parts (spark plugs, fan belts, nuts and bolts, etc.), empty oil cans

buckets, brushes, sponges

spray bottles, towels or cloths

toy gas pump, toy telephone

toy cars and trucks

tricycles and wagons

play money

clipboards, paper, pencils

warranty books, new car brochures (available at car dealerships)

auto parts catalogs (available at auto parts stores)

road maps

tire pump, tire repair kit

Construction Materials

tagboard, poster board

cardboard box

yarn

construction paper, white paper

hole punch, scissors, craft knife, stapler

tape, glue

markers, crayons

Related Units

Machines

Conservation

Oil and Gas

Energy

Tools

Careers

Pattern Directions

License Plate: Duplicate enough license plate patterns on tagboard to give one to each child. Cut out the patterns. Have the children color the license plates and write numbers on them. Punch two holes at the top of each plate and thread with yarn. Tie the plates to tricycles and wagons.

Service Checklist: Make several copies of the service checklist pattern and place each on a clipboard. Have the children check off appropriate repair work as it is completed.

Claim Ticket: Duplicate several copies of the claim ticket pattern. Cut the tickets apart or have the children cut them apart. Cut a slit on each slanted dotted line and around the circle. When a customer brings a vehicle to the repair shop to be serviced, the service manager can write a number on both parts of the ticket and then cut the ticket along the straight dotted line. The customer keeps the smaller part of the ticket until the vehicle is repaired, and the manager hangs the larger part on the tricycle to identify it.

Inspection Checklist: Make several copies of the inspection checklist pattern and place each on a cupboard door or clipboard. Have the children write on a checklist or check off each item as they inspect a vehicle.

Checkbook: See the pattern and its directions in the Shopping kit.

Credit Card: See the pattern and its directions in the Shopping kit.

Prop Directions

Shop Signs: Cut poster board into 9" x 28" sections or car-theme shapes. Write the name of a car wash or auto repair shop on each section.

Make-a-Hat (Visor)

For each hat, cut two $1\frac{1}{2}$" x 12" construction paper strips to form each hat-band. Staple the strips together so they fit a child's head. Trace the visor pattern onto construction paper to make a hat for each child and cut out, or let the children cut the patterns out. Have the children draw pictures on the visors to decorate them. Cut slits where indicated and help the children fold and glue the visors to the inside of the hatbands.

License Plate

Service Checklist

Customer's Name _____

flat tire

gas

wash

wax

vacuum

oil

Claim Ticket

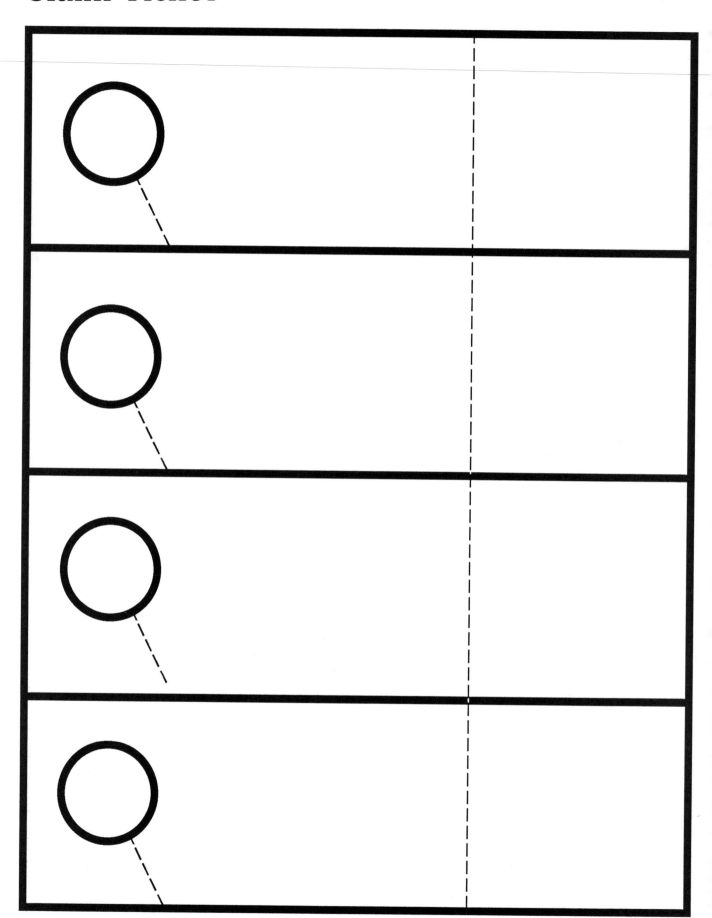

Inspection Checklist

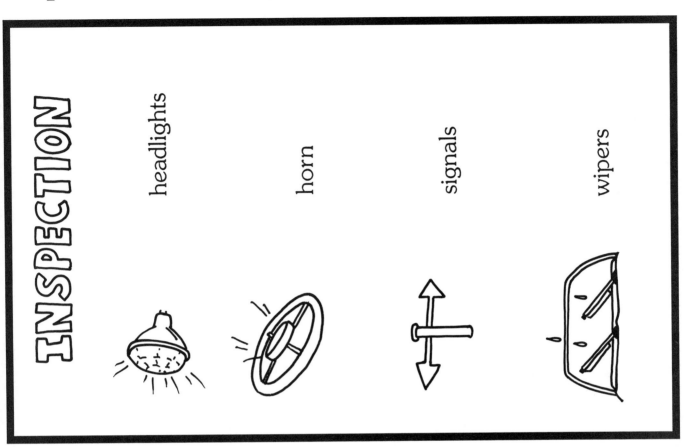

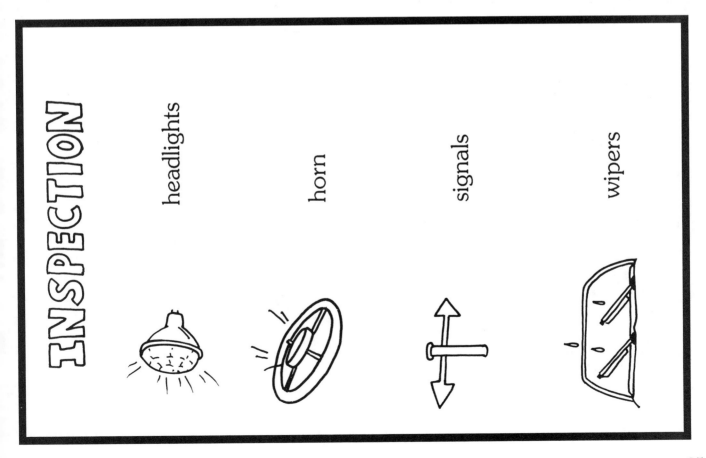

Visor

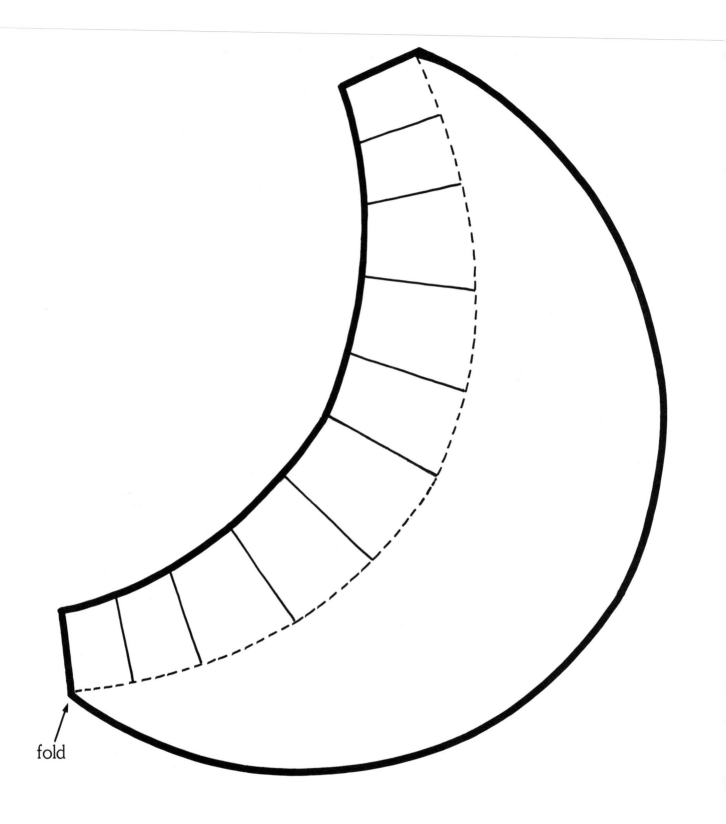

fold

Restaurant PlayKit

Overview

The Restaurant PlayKit includes the ideas and reproducibles you need to set up a play restaurant. With the materials you and the children gather and make (lists follow), you can create a fancy restaurant or a fast-food eatery.

To create a fancy restaurant, lay pieces of fabric or tablecloths on the floor. Have the children set tables or desks with copies of the place mat pattern, eating utensils, salt and pepper shakers, napkins, and vases with plastic flowers. Place a toy cash register and copies of the menu pattern on a sturdy cardboard box in a reservations area. Set up a cardboard box stove, light-weight pots and pans, cookbooks, a recipe file, and plastic plates, glasses, and food in a kitchen area.

Then encourage the children to play. Hosts and hostesses can make reservations and show customers to their tables. Waitresses and waiters can write or draw pictures of meal orders. Chefs can cook delicious food. Customers can eat, then pay their bills.

To create a fast-food restaurant, set up a cardboard order counter. Place clean, empty food containers, bags for take-out, and napkins from a local fast-food spot under the counter. Let the children make and post a restaurant sign and a menu similar to those at fast-food eateries.

Related Books

Animal Cafe by John Stadler (Checkerboard, 1987).

Benny Bakes a Cake by Eve Rice (Morrow, 1988).

Clifford's Manners by Norman Bridwell (Scholastic, 1987).

Curious George and the Pizza by H. A. Rey (Houghton Mifflin, 1985).

Frog Goes to Dinner by Mercer Mayer (Dial, 1974).

I Want to Be a Waitress by Eugene Baker (Childrens Press, 1972).

In the Night Kitchen by Maurice Sendak (Harper Junior, 1985).

Jim's Dog Muffins by Miriam Cohen (Dell, 1988).

The Milk Makers by Gail Gibbons (Macmillan, 1985).

More Spaghetti, I Say by Rita Gelman (Scholastic, 1977).

My First Baking Book by Rena Coyl (Workman, 1988).

Robbery at the Diamond Dog Diner by Eileen Christelow (Houghton Mifflin, 1988).

Materials

Ready-made Props

plastic dishes, glasses

eating utensils, cooking utensils, salt and pepper shakers

clean, empty fast-food restaurant containers and bags

pots and pans

trays

paper or cloth napkins, fast-food restaurant napkins

plastic food

vases with plastic flowers

toy cash register, play money

pencils and pens

chalkboard and chalk (for noting specials)

fabric pieces or tablecloths

dress-up clothes (especially purses and wallets)

toy highchairs, dolls

cookbooks, index cards and recipe file

Construction Materials

large fabric pieces (cotton is best)

stapler, scissors, craft knife

construction paper (including white), white paper, poster board

cardboard boxes

ribbon

needle and thread

glue

markers, crayons

tempera paint, brushes

laminating materials or clear Contact paper

Related Units

Manners

Nutrition

Mathematics
(one-to-one correspondence)

Community Workers

Money

Economics

Pattern Directions

Place Mat: Make copies of the place mat pattern on construction paper. Cut out and laminate or cover with clear Contact paper.

Order Pad: Duplicate the order pad pattern on white paper. Cut the patterns out and staple them together in sets of eight or ten to form pads. Tell the children to write down foods as they're ordered or draw pictures of them.

Reservation Book: Duplicate the reservation book pattern and cut the patterns out. Staple the pages together in sets of six or eight to make reservation books. The host or hostess or the customers may write customer names on the sheets when they make a reservation for a meal.

Menu: Make several copies of the menu patterns on construction paper. Cut them out and staple sets of two together, blank sides out. Encourage the children to write or dictate the names of foods to include on the menu. Write the name of the restaurant on the front of each menu and let the children decorate.

Credit Card: See the pattern and its directions in the Shopping kit.

Prop Directions

Restaurant Sign: Cut poster board into a 9" x 28" sign. Write the name of the restaurant on the sign.

Open/Closed Sign: Cut poster board into a 5" x 8" sign. Write "Open" on one side and "Closed" on the other.

Stove-top Box: Have the children paint a large cardboard box. Cut four six-inch circles from construction paper. Draw concentric circles on the cutout circles to look like burners. Glue the burners to the top of the box. Use the box as a stove top and to store restaurant props.

Aprons: Cut large pieces of fabric into apron shapes large enough for the children to wear. Sew a piece of ribbon to each of the top two apron corners to form straps. Sew a piece of ribbon to each side of the apron to make ties.

Make-a-Hat (Chef's Hat)
For each hat, cut out two 4" x 12" strips of white construction paper. Fold the strips in half lengthwise to form two 2" x 12" strips. Staple the ends of the strips together to form a band that will fit around a child's head. Then trace the chef's hat pattern onto white construction paper and cut out. Insert the chef's hat into the open folds of the paper strip band and glue shut.

Place Mat

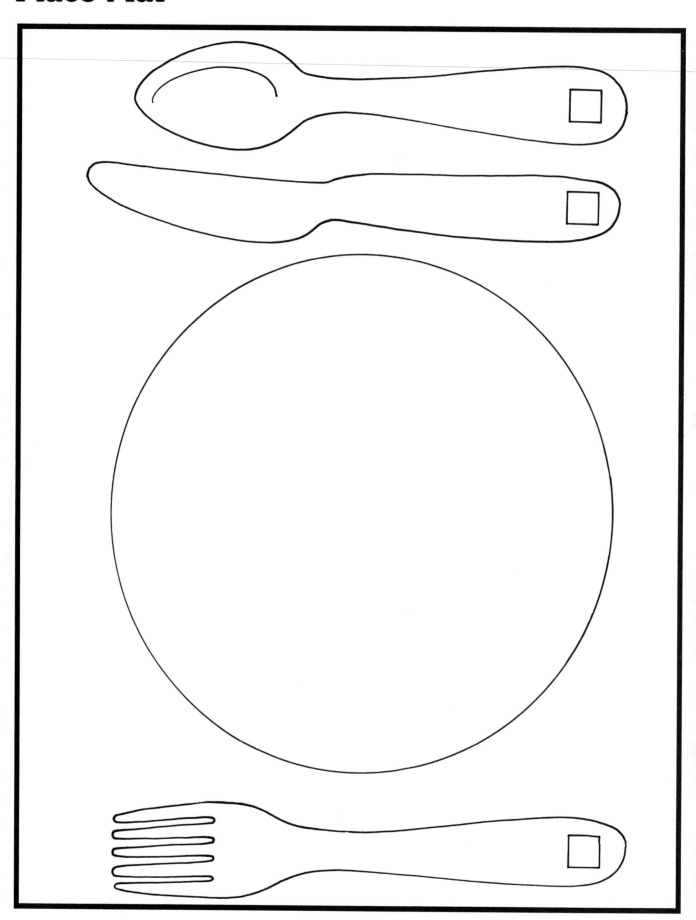

Order Pad

Order # _____

Order # _____

Order # _____

Order # _____

Reservation Book

RESERVATIONS   Day _____

Time	Name

RESERVATIONS   Day _____

Time	Name

Menu

Beverages

Desserts

Appetizers

Entrees

Chef's Hat

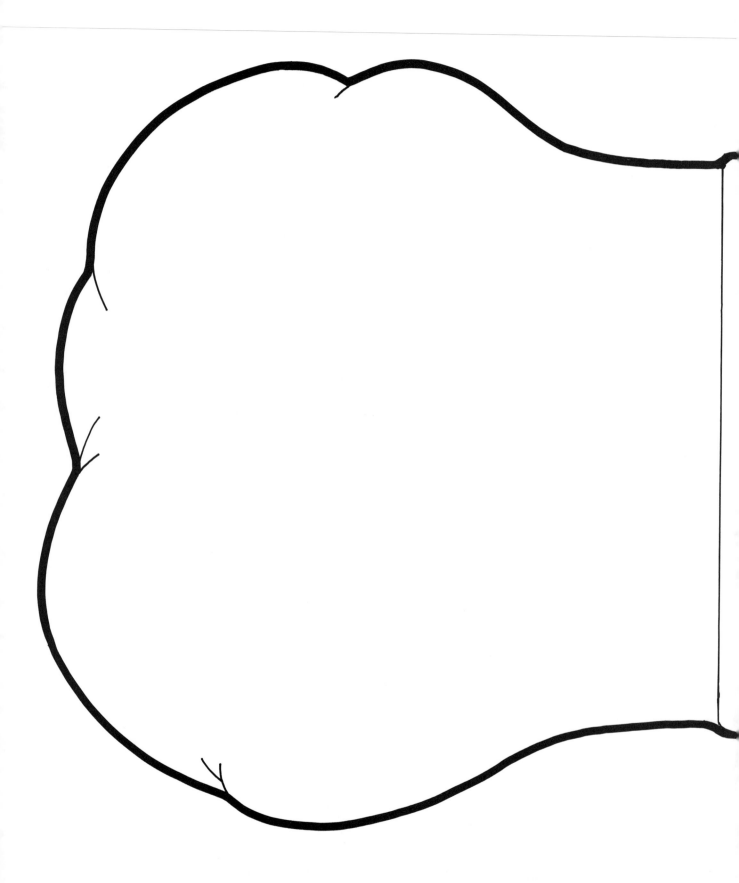

Office PlayKit

Overview

The Office PlayKit contains the ideas and reproducibles you need to provide students with creative office play. With the materials you and the children gather and make (lists follow), you can set up an office, bank, even a library or post office.

To create an office, arrange chairs around several cardboard box desks. On the desks place toy telephones, toy typewriters, file boxes, and file baskets. Also provide several kinds of paper, message pads made from the pattern, index cards, pens, and other desk equipment. Then encourage the children to play. They can answer the telephones and take messages, write on and file index cards, make appointments, write memos, and type letters. They will also enjoy sorting mail, opening letters, stamping or writing the day's date on letters, and distributing mail.

To create a bank, make a teller's window out of a large appliance box. Place chairs around a cardboard desk. Provide play money, deposit slips, checks made from the pattern in the Shopping kit, and credit applications. Then encourage the children to cash checks, deposit money into a savings account, or take out a loan.

To make a library, gather books and display them on a cardboard librarian's desk. Let the children check out the books. For a post office, save junk mail and set up a mail room counter. Put out a number of shoe boxes in which the children can sort the mail.

Related Books

Clifford Gets a Job by Norman Bridwell (Scholastic, 1985).

Curious George Takes a Job by H. A. Rey (Houghton Mifflin, 1974).

I Like the Library by Anne Rockwell (Dutton, 1977).

I Want to Be a Bank Teller by Eugene Baker (Childrens Press, 1972).

Please, Thanks, I'm Sorry by Jane Belk Moncure (Dandelion Press, 1972).

Postal Workers from A to Z by Jean Johnson (Walker, 1987).

When We Grow Up by Anne Rockwell (Dutton, 1981).

Materials

Ready-made Props

briefcases

toy telephone, toy typewriter

typing paper, index cards, legal-size yellow pads

stapler, scissors, hole punch, pencil sharpener

pens, pencils

stamps, stamp pads

rulers

tape

manila folders, envelopes

file boxes

nameplate holders

paperweights

telephone books, books

rolodex

paper clips

dress-up clothes

play money, deposit slips

shoe boxes

junk mail

Construction Materials

cardboard boxes, appliance boxes

construction paper, white paper

tagboard, poster board

tape, glue

scissors, craft knife

markers

stapler

Related Units

Feelings

Telephone Etiquette

Communication

Manners

Money

Pattern Directions

Telephone Message Pad: Make several copies of the telephone message pattern. Cut them apart, then staple them together in sets of eight to ten to form pads. Encourage the children to write messages or make picture messages on the pads.

Appointment Book: Duplicate a number of copies of the appointment book pattern. Cut the patterns apart and staple several together to form appointment books. The children can write down appointments or draw appropriate pictures at the different time slots.

Prop Directions

Office Sign: Cut a 9" x 18" poster board sign. Have the children decide on an office name and write the name on the sign. Tape the sign to the desk in the play area.

Nameplates: Cut enough 3" x 8" pieces of tagboard to give one to each child. Have each child write his or her name on a nameplate and put it into a nameplate holder. The children can keep their nameplates on their desks.

Desks: Cut out the bottom of each of several cardboard boxes. Cut a large half-circle in both sides of each box so boxes can rest on the children's legs.

Make-a-Hat (Business Owner's Hat)

For each hat, fold a 12" x 17" piece of construction paper in half to make an 8½" x 12" piece. Place the business owner's hat pattern on the fold of the construction paper as indicated on the pattern. Cut out along the solid line and open out the construction paper. Cut out the inner right side of the hat, leaving only the brim. Place the pattern back on the paper along the fold and cut along the two short dotted lines. Fold the crown back and round the corners. Trace and cut out the feather pattern, then glue the feather to the crown of the hat.

Telephone Message Pad

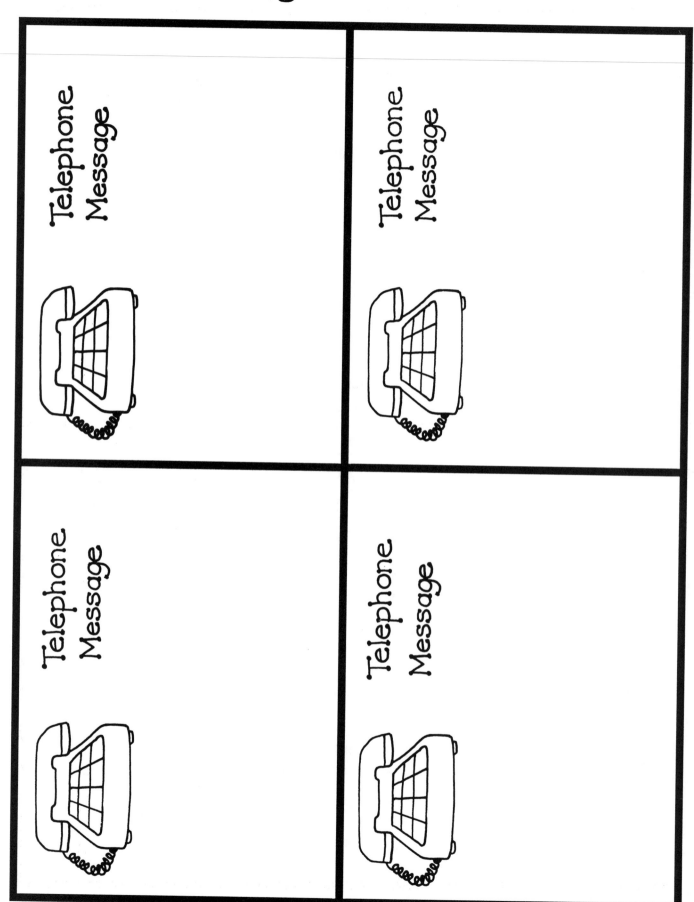

Appointment Book

APPOINTMENTS

Day _____

10:00 a.m.

11:00 a.m.

12:00 p.m.

1:00 p.m.

2:00 p.m.

3:00 p.m.

4:00 p.m.

5:00 p.m.

APPOINTMENTS

Day _____

10:00 a.m.

11:00 a.m.

12:00 p.m.

1:00 p.m.

2:00 p.m.

3:00 p.m.

4:00 p.m.

5:00 p.m.

Business Owner's Hat

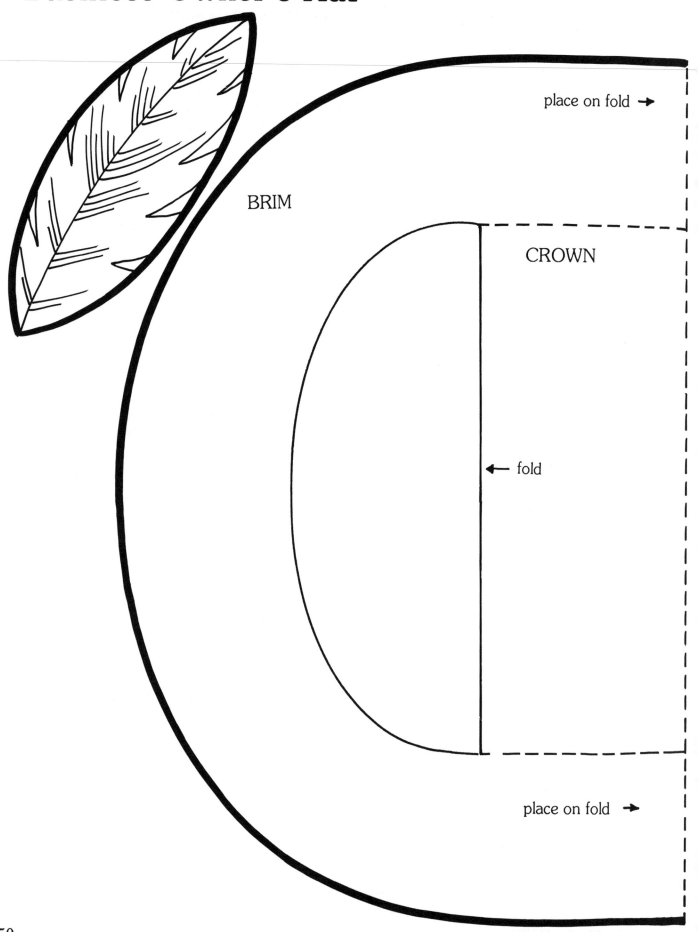

BRIM

CROWN

place on fold ➡

← fold

place on fold ➡

Construction PlayKit

Overview

The Construction PlayKit provides the ideas and reproducibles you need to involve the students in exciting construction play. With the materials you and the children gather and make (lists follow), you can set up a construction site for building roads or houses.

To create a home construction site, fill tool chests or tackle boxes with building tools (small hammers, screwdrivers, pliers, sandpaper, etc.). Make blocks, clipboards and paper, old blueprints, and scrap lumber available. Also provide clean, empty paint cans and paintbrushes. Set up a cardboard box desk with a toy telephone in a construction office area.

Then encourage the children to play. Architects can meet with clients, draw house plans, and read blueprints. Carpenters can make houses from blocks or lumber scraps; with close adult supervision carpenters can hammer and use screwdrivers. Contractors can make company signs, use the telephone to order building supplies, and pay bills.

For a road construction site, set out blocks, toy trucks and cars, and toy traffic signs. Let the children use a red flag (see the directions for making one under "Prop Directions") to direct traffic. Construction workers will enjoy building roads and moving traffic.

Related Books

Big Wheels by Anne Rockwell (Dutton, 1986).

Building a House by Byron Barton (Greenwillow, 1981).

Curious George and the Dump Truck by Margaret Rey (Houghton Mifflin, 1984).

Drill, Pump, Fill by Tana Hoban (Greenwillow, 1975).

I Read Signs by Tana Hoban (Morrow, 1983).

Katy and the Big Snow by Virginia Burton (Houghton, 1942).

The Little House by Virginia Burton (Houghton, 1942).

Machines by Anne and Harlow Rockwell (Macmillan, 1972).

Machines at Work by Byron Barton (Crowell, 1987).

Mike Mulligan and the Steam Shovel by Virginia Burton (Houghton Mifflin, 1939).

Roads by Gail Gibbons (Crowell, 1983).

Thruway by Anne and Harlow Rockwell (Macmillan, 1972).

The Tool Box by Anne Rockwell (Macmillan, 1972).

Up Goes the Skyscraper by Gail Gibbons (Four Winds, 1986).

Materials

Ready-made Props

tools (small hammers, screwdrivers, wrenches, pliers, rulers, sandpaper, levels, etc.)

paintbrushes; clean, empty paint cans; paint stirrers; paint chips (available from paint stores)

tool or tackle boxes

carpenter's aprons and belts

blocks

lumber scraps (soft pine works best)

nuts, bolts, screws

old blueprints

toy trucks, cars, tractors, traffic signs

hardware catalogs and brochures

clipboards, paper, pencils

toy telephone

Construction Materials

newspaper torn into 2" strips

liquid starch

balloons

paint, paintbrushes, paint stirrers

tagboard; construction paper, including red and yellow

red fabric

rubber cement, glue

$\frac{1}{2}$" wooden dowel

scissors, stapler

markers, crayons

saw

pan or bowl

cardboard box

Related Units

Jobs

Tools

Machines

Cities and Towns

Working Together

Pattern Directions

Materials Order Form: Make several copies of the order form pattern and place each on a clipboard. Encourage the children to write down or draw pictures of building materials they want to order.

Bill: Make several copies of the bill pattern and cut them apart. Place each bill on a clipboard. Let the children make up bills for materials they order.

Prop Directions

Stop Sign and Slow Sign: Cut a 9" octagon shape from red construction paper and one from yellow construction paper. Write "STOP" on the red shape, "SLOW" on the yellow shape. Staple the shapes back to back. Glue a paint stirrer to the base for a handle. Let the children use the traffic signs to direct traffic.

Red Flag: Cut a 15" x 17" section from a piece of red fabric. Saw a $\frac{1}{2}$" dowel to a 24" length. Staple the top of the red cloth around the dowel, letting the rest of the cloth hang down. Tell the children to use the red flag to direct traffic.

Make-a-Hat (Hard Hat)

For each hat, blow up a balloon to the approximate size of a child's head. On tagboard, trace and cut out the visor pattern from the Auto Repair kit. Cut slits in the visor as shown on the pattern. Attach the visor to the middle of the balloon with rubber cement. Then pour liquid starch into a pan or bowl. Help the children dip newspaper strips into the starch and lay them on the top of the balloon and the visor; cover those areas with several layers of strips. Let the newspaper dry completely. Next, pop the balloon and trim off any excess newspaper to form a hard hat. Then let the children paint their hats as they like. For added detail, duplicate copies of the construction symbol patterns on construction paper. Help the children cut out the symbols, then let them color and glue them to their hats.

Materials Order Form

Order Form

Price	Description	Quantity

Bill

BILL

Materials _____

Labor _____

Total _____

BILL

Materials _____

Labor _____

Total _____

BILL

Materials _____

Labor _____

Total _____

BILL

Materials _____

Labor _____

Total _____

Construction Symbols

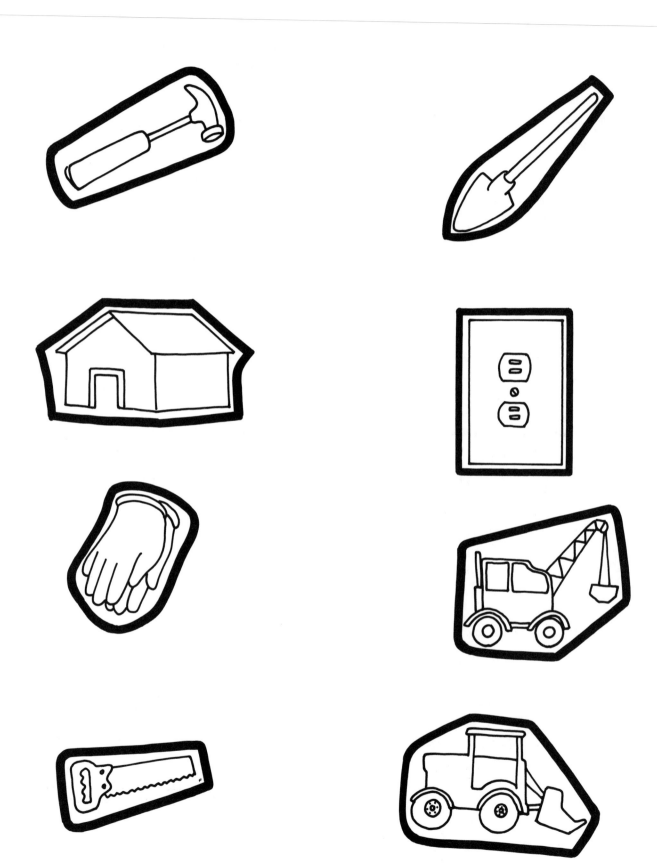

TV Station PlayKit

Overview

The TV Station PlayKit includes the ideas and reproducibles you need to provide creative broadcasting play. With the materials you and the children gather and make (lists follow), you can create either a TV station or a radio station.

To set up a TV station, turn a cardboard box into a "nightly news" desk. Follow the directions under "Prop Directions" to construct a camera, and set it out. Place a flannel board behind the news desk and cover it with news and weather items such as sports pictures, maps, articles, cooking utensils, weather symbols, and so on. Place a toy tape recorder with a microphone on the desk.

Then encourage the children to play. They can pretend to be newscasters, weather people, camera people, directors, crew members, and celebrities. Children can operate the camera, read the news, give sports scores, forecast the weather, and interview famous people: sports heroes, rock stars, even the president. A child might want to play at being a TV chef and demonstrate how to make a special dish.

To create a radio station, ask the children to bring in favorite tapes and records. Set out a child's tape recorder or record player on a table and let the students take turns at playing DJ. Listeners can use toy telephones to call in requests for special songs, and sing along. Between songs, the DJ can give news briefs and announcers can broadcast commercials.

Related Books

Anna, Grandpa and the Big Storm by Carla Stevens (Puffin, 1986).

Backyard Basketball Superstar by Monica Klein (Pantheon, 1981).

Clifford Goes to Hollywood by Norman Bridwell
    (Scholastic, 1986).

One Wet Jacket by Nancy Tafuri (Morrow, 1988).

Rain by Peter Speir (Doubleday, 1982).

Ramona: Behind the Scenes of a Television Show by Elaine Scott
    (Morrow, 1988).

Snow by Isao Sasaki (Viking, 1982).

Sports by Michael Ricketts (Wonder, 1977).

A Summer Day by Douglas Florian (Morrow, 1988).

What Goes on at a Radio Station? by Susan Gilmore
    (CarolRhoda Books, 1984).

A Winter Day by Douglas Florian (Morrow, 1987).

Materials

Ready-made Props

dress-up clothes (including suit coats, ties, dresses)

child's tape recorder and microphone, child's record player

toy telephones

computer paper

sports hats (baseball caps, football helmets, etc.)

sports equipment (baseballs, tennis racquets, etc.)

sports and news magazines, television guides, newspapers

chef's hat, cooking utensils

maps

typewriter

chalkboard and chalk

flannel board, flannel letters and numbers

clipboards, pens and pencils

Construction Materials

tagboard or poster board, construction paper, large sheets of paper

cardboard boxes

shoe boxes

flannel

3-foot length of elastic, ribbon

paper towel tubes

black paint, paintbrushes

markers (including red)

stapler, scissors, hole punch, craft knife

laminating materials or clear Contact paper

glue, tape

Related Units

Sports

Weather

Careers

People in the News

Current Events

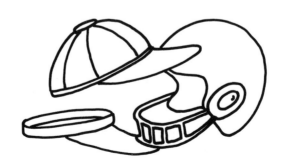

Pattern Directions

U.S. Weather Map: Enlarge the U.S. weather map pattern and trace it onto a piece of flannel. Cut the shape out and place it on a flannel board behind the news desk.

Weather Symbols: Cut out the different patterns and trace them onto different colors of flannel. Cut out the symbols and have the children put them on the flannel weather map to forecast the weather. Let the children add flannel numbers and letters as needed.

Sports Symbols: Cut out the different patterns and trace them onto different colors of flannel. Cut the symbols out. Encourage the children to put the pieces on the flannel board, along with flannel numbers, as they give the sports report.

Thermometer: Cut a 20" x 15" piece from poster board. Duplicate the two halves of the thermometer pattern and glue them onto the poster board. Cut a slit in the two places marked on the pattern. Thread a length of elastic through the slits and staple the ends together in the back. Use a marker to color half the elastic red. Show the children how to move the elastic up and down to indicate different temperatures.

Prop Directions

Crew List: Use a large sheet of paper and a marker to make a list of people who might work on a television news show: camera person, producer, director, newscaster, weather person, sportscaster, and so on. Write a child's name next to each position. Post the list.

Camera: For each camera, paint a child's shoe box and a paper towel tube black. Cut a hole a bit wider than the paper towel tube in each end of the box. Slide the tube through the holes for a viewer.

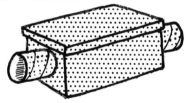

Make-a-Hat (Weather Hat)

For each hat, cut a 12" circle from tagboard or poster board. Laminate the circle or cover it with clear Contact paper. Cut through the circle from one edge to the center. Overlap the edges and staple together. Punch two holes in each side of the hat. Thread ribbon through each set of holes and knot to form ties. Trace the weather symbol patterns onto construction paper and let the children cut them out. The children can tape the appropriate symbol to the hat to indicate the day's forecast.

U.S. Weather Map

Weather Symbols

Sports Symbols

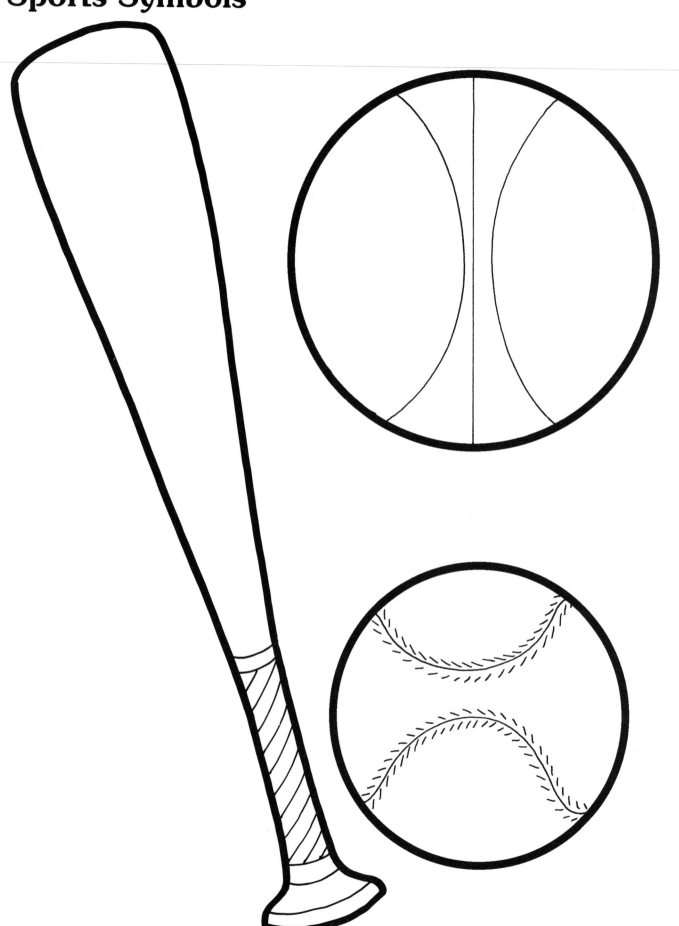

Sports Symbols

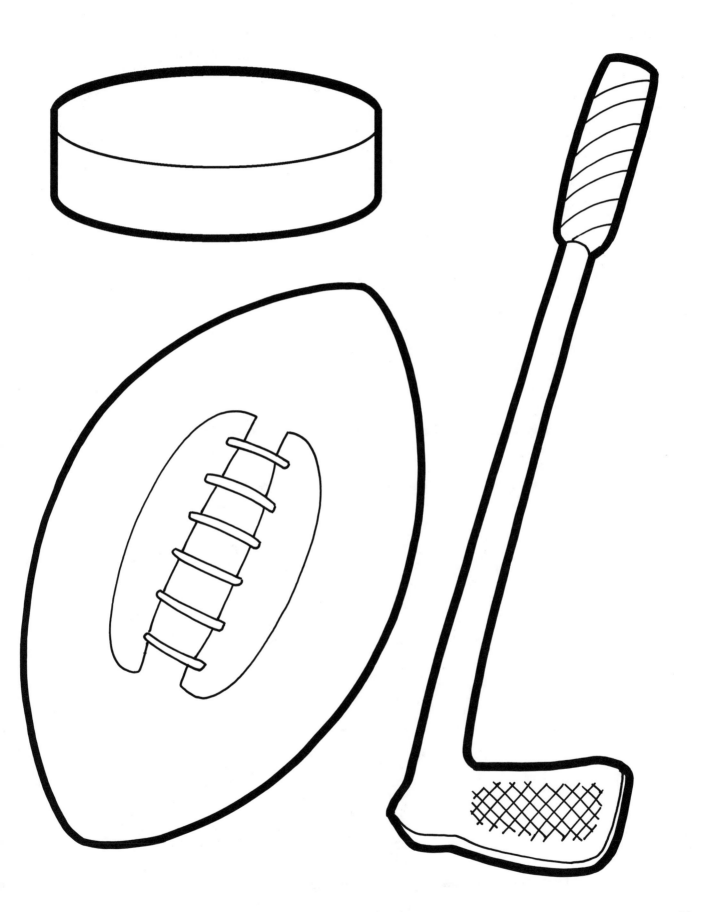

Thermometer

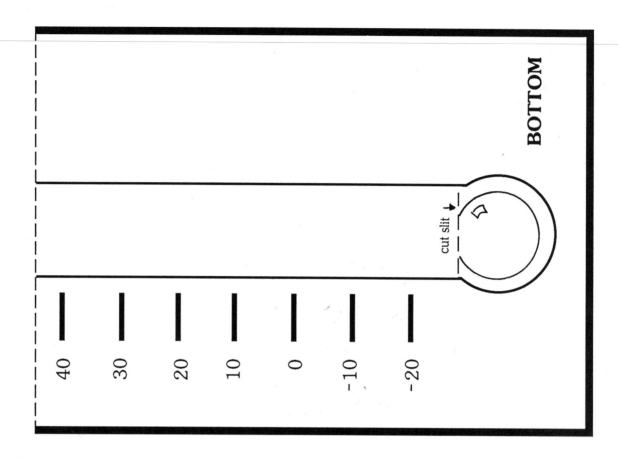

BOTTOM

cut slit

40

30

20

10

0

-10

-20

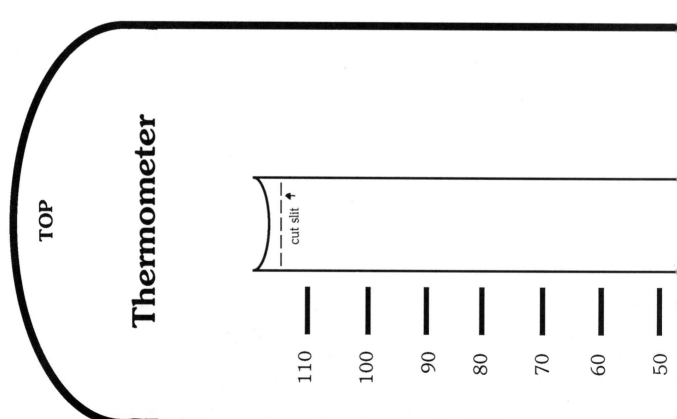

TOP

Thermometer

cut slit

110

100

90

80

70

60

50